Mastering the Pain

Overcoming Through Self Care

Meosha Culpepper

Copyright © 2021 by BUT GOD! Publishings

All rights reserved. No part of this book may be used or reproduced by any means, graphic, electronic, or mechanical, including photocopying, recording, taping, or by any information storage retrieval system, without the written permission of the publisher except in the case of brief quotations embodied in critical articles and reviews.

Disclaimer

This book is not intended to diagnose or treat medical nor psychological conditions. This book is to bring education and awareness to those who are providing care and services to others.

CONTENTS

Introduction 1

Unapologetically Me 4

This is for You 11

Vicarious Trauma 14

Secondary Traumatic Stress..18

Compassion Fatigue...22

Burnout..26

Self-Care 31

A Call to Action...39

References 44

Introduction

Have you ever felt a moment of fear and anticipation when a situation takes you to an emotional place that causes your heart rate to elevate? How about an experience that triggered your fight-or-flight response and may have caused a feeling of panic?

There are times in life where you or someone you know may relate to the experience in these questions. In the world we live in today, especially with the COVID pandemic, many of us are dealing with circumstances causing internal stress. Despite the stress, we often push ourselves to move forward due to life's responsibilities.

The pandemic has destroyed our normal way of life and pushed our society into a "new norm," but production and services must still take place in this world. The workforce and company business functions are essential in keeping basic needs met and desires fulfilled. It takes people, places, and things to keep this world going around, no matter the unexpected changes that take place here on earth. My husband is a truck driver, and without him and other drivers transporting products, we wouldn't receive the things we need at home such as toilet paper, water, food, etc. Consider the essential workers, medical workers, first responders, teachers, ministers, praise leaders, mental health professionals, caregivers, and so many other necessary leaders. People in these positions have given their lives serving in their professions.

Each of these workers is at risk of burnout, vicarious trauma, secondary traumatic stress, compassion fatigue, and just straight up exhaustion. Because of the stress that these positions can attract, some of these workers deal with spiritual bleeding, financial difficulties, and even physical health concerns. They put their lives on the line for others but rarely have a place to go and become refueled, refreshed, and rejuvenated.

I'm passionate about this topic because of my experience as an Emergency Response Children's Social Worker (ER CSW). The stress that I faced with every investigation began to take a toll on my body physically. I was having panic attacks, chills and sweats, hyperventilation, vomiting, dizzy spells, and severe body pains. Every time I went to the hospital, they said nothing was wrong with me until one doctor told me it wasn't a physical issue but a stress-induced psychological issue. That was the beginning of my self care journey, and it changed my life. I am still currently an ER CSW and I schedule self care into my lifestyle because of the stress I encounter on the job.

Is there a place for essential workers to go to become refueled, refreshed, and rejuvenated? Where can they turn when they have no one to serve them when they're in need? Who can they talk to when in crisis? When their cup is half full or even empty, how are they supposed to refuel from the feelings of overwhelm, exhaustion, and burnout?

In this book, we'll discuss the details of my passion for faith leaders in the marketplace and in ministry. This book is not intended to diagnose or treat medical nor psychological conditions but to bring education and awareness to those who are providing care to others. This burning passion within led me into launching a 501c3 nonprofit organization, Times of Expression & Refreshing (TER) Ministries, Inc. It is my heart's desire to serve leaders who are working in the community and within the marketplace as a leader of faith. This book won't be for everyone. It is focused on those who are leading while spiritually or emotionally bleeding. It is my hope that after you read this book, you will understand the importance of applying self care to your daily schedule and recognize the signs of vicarious trauma, secondary traumatic stress, compassion fatigue, and burnout.

Before we get into the meat of this book, I'd love to introduce myself.

Unapologetically Me

Hi! It's Meosha here. I express myself best through writing, so why not put it in a book? In this journey called life, I have struggled to find the attention needed to reach my goals. It seems as if everyone is in competition with one another. I rarely see brother helping brother, let alone strangers helping strangers. It's as if everyone is in their own little worlds, but it doesn't have to be that way.

The change starts with me. It starts with you, and the impact starts with us.

So who am I? I am just a regular person who loves seeing the needs of others fulfilled. I get myself into trouble at times because I go above and beyond for others to make sure they have what they need to get to the next level in life. It doesn't matter if the need is spiritual, physical, financial, or even psychological; with all the passion I have within, I try to figure out how can I make someone's life better.

I was told once that I'm a jack of all trades but not sure what to become the master of. That statement has never left my mind. It catapulted me into looking deeper into my journey and I have often asked myself, 'What is your purpose?' I've looked within to search for the answer and have begun repositioning my way of thinking and my focus of each day.

I am a Jesus freak, a wife, a mother, an emergency response children's social worker, an ordained pastor, a dance coordinator, and an introvert at heart. Others may have a different definition, but I have come to accept myself and what I have to offer this world.

Jesus freak? Yes, I said it. I am a Jesus freak because I have come to know who Jesus is. I didn't grow up in church, so Jesus wasn't spoken of in my household. I came to know who Jesus really was during a domestic violence incident at the age of 19. The guy I was dating at that time came home one night drunk and demanded sex. He stood over me as I lay in bed and began to touch me. I continuously told him to stop and then I kicked him away from me. That's when he began to beat me. He punched me in my face and then threw me to the floor. He kneeled on top of me with one knee in my chest and the other on my throat, and then he banged my head against the floor.

Eventually, he let me up because he needed to use the restroom. I didn't have a phone in the house, so I reached for his cell phone. As he walked out of the restroom, he appeared angrier. He went into the closet, took out his belt, and wrapped it around his hand with the belt buckle exposed. Just as he raised his hand up, I yelled, "In the name of Jesus, make him stop!"

The belt fell to the floor, he fell on his knees, and tears fell from his eyes. He begged for forgiveness, and it was then that I knew Jesus was real. Because of that night, no other religion or non-religious person can convince me that Jesus is not significant. After all the yelling and screaming I did, nothing changed until I cried out His name. That's why I say that I am a Jesus freak. I can go on all day talking about Him, but I will move to my next point for now.

At the time of this book's release, I have been a wife for a little over four years. I never thought I would get married. I never wanted to get married nor expected to be married. But because of all that I went through, I now know it shaped me into who I am, and I was created just for him. Big Man! My husband, Mr. Culpepper. I never thought in my life that someone would ever want to marry me. I have always been the person who walked alone, nervous of a crowd. Mr. Culpepper was definitely molded for me. He is patient, loving, kind, long suffering indeed, and gentle. I can go on and on about this man. God prepared me to be a wife, and Mr. Culpepper is pulling out of me the wife I was destined to be just for him. I will spare the details for another book.

I am also the mother of a beautiful adult, Generation Z, daughter. She is so amazing and dear to my heart! I am so grateful for God trusting me with such a blessing. Was I perfect as a mother? NO. If there was a mother manual, I would have had it glued to my hand. I wasn't just a mother—I was a single mother. That's another book all by itself. I have also upgraded to be blessed with bonus adult children. Family is a beautiful thing to have in life, and I am so grateful for being chosen for the life I have with my family.

I am an Emergency Response Children's Social Worker (ER CSW) and I love it. What is an ER CSW? In a nutshell, I would say a "baby snatcher." I say that jokingly because during my first year of being in the field, I ran into several parents who described us to be just that. But we are more than just baby snatchers. ER CSWs are a unique breed of social workers who investigate the abuse and neglect of children. It is our job to make sure that children are safe within their homes. It hasn't always been easy, and the media doesn't help. It has taken a lot of sweat and tears, but it has all been worth it. To be honest, my experience as an ER CSW is the main reason I'm writing this book. I never discuss anything about what I do as an ER CSW, and I don't ever believe I ever will, but I will be sharing the effects that I've overcome and those I'm still coming through as an ER CSW. Keep reading and you will find out what I mean.

Mastering the Pain

As of 2019, I am an ordained pastor. When some hear the word pastor, they may cringe or grind their teeth. It may be because of old religious beliefs or maybe not so much of any tradition. The journey hasn't always been easy, but I've always known the call was on my life. Before I knew who God was, He and I would have private conversations. When the ordination took place for me to become a pastor, it confirmed all the crises I had to go through to get to the position. The title doesn't define who I am; it's for the purpose and assignment that is my life. The ordination had to take place because of where my journey is headed.

I have been a dance coordinator at my local church since 2012. Anyone who knows me knows that I am passionate about dance ministry. I have been a prophetic dancer since 2000, and I have learned a lot in ministry throughout the years. Dance started out as therapy for me, and then it elevated to becoming a leader of it. Never in my wildest dreams did I think I would lead in ministry, but I love being a student for life and serving others in their vision. When I was given this responsibility, I was excited and nervous. You see, at the time I was homeless. Four months after accepting the call to be the dance coordinator, I ended up in a car accident that left me with seven herniated discs throughout my neck and back areas. Because I am a fighter and will never quit, I pushed through the physical and emotional pain while living in a shelter as an injured, unemployed single mother. I was tried in the fire of life, but I praise God for bringing me through the process and leading me to where I am today in Him.

I am an introvert at heart! I never knew what that word was until my pastor had us take a personality test. Then I understood why I was shy and nervous in crowds. The average person wouldn't think I was, but it takes a lot for me to prepare myself to be out in a crowd of people. When I perform, I get home and feel physically drained, but I believe this ties into my gift as an Empath as well. Behind my shyness, I have a strong energy to confront and impose rulership. I have a bit of a hard edge because I am not afraid to question someone who is trying to misuse or bully another person. My drive is justification on behalf of others. In today's world, we must understand what people are about and what they stand for, and this is where my advocating character as a social worker comes out. Some say that I can be confrontational, but my purpose is always helping others.

In 2021, I earned my master's in social work. I suffered through pain, sweat, and tears for my degree and I now understand why others boldly carry the letters after their names. It takes a lot to receive a higher education, and I applaud every person who sacrifices their time, family, life, and income to further their education. It took me three long years to earn my master's, and that is where my self care journey began. Before we learn more about self care, though, I want to take a moment to define who this book is for. Let's dive in!

This is for You

This book is for you, the one who feels that you are pouring from an empty or a half-full cup. You feel like if you push one more time, you may not have any more to give. You need a break and a place where you know it's okay to not be okay. A place where you're given the opportunity to recognize what is really going on psychologically and receive a better understanding on how to handle the feelings of burnout.

Does this sound like you or someone you know? You may be able to relate to Elijah in the Bible. Elijah was obedient to what was spoken to him by God. He obeyed and did what the Lord had assigned him to do despite being called names and being threatened by his enemy Jezebel. Elijah obeyed every command the Lord told him. However, because Elijah neglected to take care of himself by not eating and getting the proper rest needed, he allowed the words of his enemy to consume his emotional state to the point where he allowed the words of someone else to make him feel less than and caused him to have suicidal ideations.

You may be the person, or you may know a person, who is blameless and upright like Job in the Bible. You may have a positive influence among family, friends, and the community. You stand up for those who should be praying and interceding for themselves. You have done so much for others, but when in a crisis, no one comes to help in your time of need.

Or are you an activist or advocator such as Shadrach, Meshach, and Abednego? The leader who will stand up for what you believe is right, ignoring the consequences it would bring to your life. You are at-risk to the feelings of being alone with no one to turn to. You have a consistent mindset through the stress of knowing that you may be destroyed for what you believe in.

You are that male, female, or gender neutral who loves Jesus and is operating in a leadership position, residing within the United States of America, who is in need of self care strategies to apply to your life in order to fully operate in your calling and purpose while here on earth. You may have gone through, will go through, or are coming out of something due to your work helping others and/or working with others.

This book is for you!

In any position helping others, there is an exposure risk of vicarious trauma, secondary traumatic stress, compassion fatigue, and burnout. You may have that call to duty of supporting a person who is actively in the middle of a crisis. Maybe you have no time to get yourself together, but must handle the situation anyway. This can have a psychological effect on you. You may have gotten to a place where you feel exhausted all the time, and everything you try to get through the exhaustion just doesn't work. You're trying to keep your head above water in your assignment, but you feel like you're drowning or emotionally sinking and just can't physically function the way you used to. Friends or colleagues confide in you, and your compassion for them isn't the same, causing you to feel emotionally numb. Maybe you have been in the same position for so long and the position is repetitively stressful. You're straight-up fatigued mentally, physically, and even emotionally, and you don't have the energy or ability to do anything at all.

With this book, I want to bring awareness and teach you to identify the signs, symptoms, prevention, and treatments for these effects. First, let's look into the awareness of vicarious trauma.

Vicarious Trauma

If you are a caregiver of a loved one, an advocate for a community, a counselor, a teacher, a preacher, or any person who tends to the needs of others, you are at risk of vicarious trauma. I will say "we" because I am in this category. We have either been exposed to or are at risk of vicarious trauma.

The following positions are individuals who are at risk of vicarious trauma: doctors, nurses, psychologists, social workers, lawyers, police, and public health workers (Lodha, 2021). It is also an occupational challenge for people working and volunteering in the victim services fields such as law enforcement, fire services, emergency medical services, and other allied professions (Sprang, 2018).

Vicarious trauma happens due to the exposure to trauma and crisis situations. It refers to an intense reaction to being exposed to another person's trauma story or exposed to the details of the traumatic event (Sprang, 2018). Vicarious trauma is when you have firsthand been exposed to someone who is in the midst of a traumatic event or have been exposed to a traumatic story that's being told where you become psychologically affected because of it. This type of exposure can cause you to become affected emotionally, behaviorally, physiologically, cognitively, and spiritually.

You may various psychological symptoms, including compassion fatigue, secondary traumatic stress, and critical incidence stress (Sprang, 2018). If you're in this category, you may feel the emotions of grief, anger, and sadness, just to name a few. During my experience with vicarious trauma, I had a hard time recognizing my emotions. I found that I was skilled at disassociating. Because of that, I was unable to activate my self-awareness until it was too late. For others, vicarious trauma can affect eating habits, sleeping patterns, or maybe even cause an increase of alcohol or substance use (Lodha, 2021).

The effects of vicarious trauma may cause manifestations through the physical body. This is what happens with me. When I investigated domestic violence referrals, by the time I left the client's home, I was sweating, tense, my stomach felt nauseous, I would be short of breath, and at times I would vomit. I used to keep barf bags in my car because I knew I would end up vomiting at least once a week. I remember a time when I was getting ready to serve a warrant for the removal of child due to parents being involved in a severe domestic violence incident. As I was in the office preparing and thinking over the reasons I would need to explain to the parents why I was removing their child from them, my cognition was affected. I was speaking with the placement worker and confirming the information needed for the new caregiver, and I had a difficult time concentrating. I began asking her questions that I already knew the answer to, and I kept asking her to repeat herself because I wasn't comprehending a word that was coming out of her mouth. It was so embarrassing. Not only did I recognize it, but she did as well. She asked me if I was okay, and about 15 minutes after that phone call, I began vomiting stomach acid. Needless to say, my duty supervisor had to call in another social worker to assist me with serving the warrant that evening due to my body having these uncontrollable physical symptoms to vicarious trauma. I remember having to contact my husband and a friend to carpool to my office and drive me home. The outcome of vicarious trauma can leave you in an unpleasant state causing you to replay the event over and over again mentally, or suppress the memory entirely, as well as avoiding anything that may make you feel like it could occur again (McAfee & Watts, 2021).

So how can we treat vicarious trauma? Some approaches include getting out of the victim's shoes, applying self care, and ensuring that you are getting enough sleep, eating healthy, and performing regular exercises (Lcsw & Sawicki, 2019). Another personal approach is intentionally engaging in activities that may make you feel good and being social, because socialization is a big asset to the mind.

There are therapeutic treatments for treating vicarious trauma which includes Trauma Focused Cognitive Behavioral Therapy. This method caters to your individual needs via a therapy plan. The therapy plan addresses distorted thinking patterns, negative reactions, and actions (Figley, 2013). It also helps identify other symptoms associated with vicarious trauma.

Another method is Eye Movement Desensitization and Reprocessing (EMDR) Therapy, which is an effective way of reducing negative feelings, thoughts, and physical sensations associated with your trauma (Figley, 2013). This is the form of therapy I was treated with. It works using a series of guided eye movements and other exercises to help you become desensitized from the traumatic event.

Coping with any form of trauma, including vicarious trauma, happens better through trauma therapy which helps prevent future occurrences. These forms of therapy may be obtained by consulting a therapist trained on trauma therapy and cognitive behavioral therapy. Vicarious trauma is something to be aware of, but it can look like secondary traumatic stress. They are not the same. Let's learn more about secondary traumatic stress.

Secondary Traumatic Stress

Secondary traumatic stress can easily be confused as vicarious trauma. Vicarious trauma is when you experience a traumatic event first hand and if affects you psychologically. As a hypothetical example, when a police officer happens to be present at an arrest where he watches his partner beaten by a criminal so brutally that it causes a psychological response. He is impacted emotionally and mentally immediately during his exposure to the person who is experiencing the trauma. Or he may have not been present at the scene but heard the details of the story and it ends up affecting him psychologically at the moment of hearing the information. Secondary traumatic stress, on the other hand, happens after being exposed trauma over a period of time and leads to feelings of helplessness, confusion, isolation, numbness or avoidance, and persistent arousal. This often happens to those who interact with traumatized individuals and experience repeated or extreme exposure to unpleasant details of traumatic events (Sprang et al., 2019).

Secondary traumatic stress is normally characterized by emotional and physical exhaustion. This leads to a decline in the ability of an individual to empathize or feel compassion for other people. Secondary traumatic stress mostly develops when you have been working with traumatized people or have been traumatized before (Steele, 2019). It is natural but can be very destructive. It greatly influences your way of doing things since you cannot withstand the stress anymore. This condition closely resembles post-traumatic stress disorder (PTSD) (Figley, 2017) and may make you unable to cope with others.

There are ways to recognize the symptoms of secondary traumatic stress. The symptoms are usually gradual and are either physical symptoms, mental, cognitive, behavioral, or a combination of many. The symptoms may cause disturbed sleep patterns because you wake up frequently due to a flight of ideas (Miller, 2021). There is a noticeable change in appetite and they can present with difficulties breathing as well as speech. It can also cause a prolonged increase in heart rate. You may isolate yourself from other people and like staying alone. You may also withdraw from routine work (Gley, 2016). You may have increased joints and muscle pain because you always feel exhausted and your brain is in an overworked state. You may present with hyper-vigilance; this means that you always stay alert. Your immune system often becomes weak, causing you to be prone to other medical conditions. Affected people become sad over minor issues and are always sad even when not provoked. They express anger and can easily fall into fights.

They have a lowered level of concentration since they have a lot of things in their mind. They cannot listen to one thing and do what is required of them (Konistan, 2017). They may feel helpless and experience rigid thinking, where they believe in what they know and do not listen to other people's ideas. They present apathy and lack of interest in activities and other people, thus always staying alone unless they're forced to socialize. Perfectionism can also present in some people (Steele, 2019).

So how can we treat secondary traumatic stress? You may recover by applying some of the following strategies: writing down all feelings, joining support groups to develop coping mechanisms, and focusing on self care (Figley, 2017). Care will include a healthy diet that is essential for brain function, exercise, and adequate sleep patterns to promote rest and brain relaxation. You can also develop new coping strategies like contemporary relaxation practices or yoga activities. This greatly contributes to muscle relaxation and reduces the probability of adverse effects (Figley, 2018). Another strategy is developing positivity toward your work to make you realize that you can be successful and bring about change. Once you start realizing the importance of help you get from other people, you invite change in yourself (Konistan, 2017).

It is wise to implement the above measures so that recovery can take place and you can realize your self-worth and value in your communities. This is a lot of information to take in, so feel free to read this book more than once. Trauma and stress are real, and we must learn to recognize it in ourselves and others. If not, it can affect our emotions, which could lead to fatigue. As a matter of fact, let's talk about compassion fatigue, shall we?

Compassion Fatigue

Compassion fatigue is a condition that refers to the state of accumulative emotional, psychological, and physical exhaustion. It causes a decrease in the ability to express compassion to others, which leads to negative caring habits. This may come about as a result of exposure to stories that are traumatic to oneself or when one is in the process of healing others and it causes strain that may in turn affect your level of performance due to daily stress (Del, 2019). Compassion fatigue is known to result from an individual trying to help those who are being traumatized or under noticeable emotional duress. Compassion fatigue affects mostly individuals in helping professions such as lawyers and many others (Crowe, 2016).

Let's discuss some symptoms of compassion fatigue. Once a person is traumatized, they are likely to present themselves differently than usual. Compassion fatigue can affect you emotionally, physically, mentally, and spiritually. The most common symptoms of compassion fatigue include negative thoughts toward work, irritability, and being prone to anger (DuBois & Mistretta, 2019). You may experience images that disrupt your normal level of function. You may start to experience problems in the way you relate with others especially at work. This is because you become emotionally detached from those you are used to relating with. You may perceive living in this world to be the most dangerous thing and become concerned with the safety of your family and yourself. A person experiencing compassion fatigue may become less productive at work and in their personal life. They lack the energy to carry out their normal activities. They are full of questions regarding their profession, their level of competence, and their effectiveness at work. The person is at risk to become addicted to drugs or alcohol, gambling programs, and may possibly be involved in dangerous activities. They may present with states of depersonalization, recurring headaches, and continued weight loss. Insomnia may also occur due to a flight of thoughts and ideas (Gottfried & Bride, 2018). Compassion fatigue has several symptoms that are a great threat to an individual, their work activities, as well as the people that they relate with in their daily living.

I remember a time in my life when I experienced compassion fatigue. I wasn't any good to anyone in my life at that time. I was emotionally numb to others and couldn't provide the compassion needed for my friends, family, and my clients. I began realizing it when someone cried and I felt no compassion for their feelings. Once I recognized my behavior and became aware of it, I did something about it. I implemented self care strategies in my daily life. My next book will go more into details about my self care strategies, so be on the look out for that!

Compassion fatigue is treatable. If you think you or a loved one may be suffering, it's wise to seek medical attention. Treatment can include self care programs (Allister, 2020). These are composed of strategies to develop good eating habits, get adequate rest, and help you develop coping mechanisms (Gottfried & Bride, 2018). The individual with this condition is advised to talk regularly to their workmates regarding the traumatizing event. By doing so, you can overcome the stress and cope and work normally. Sharing trauma promotes healing. Another way to treat compassion fatigue is through a healthy balance in relationships with other people (Taithe, 2019). A person who is healing from compassion fatigue is encouraged to learn to do less tiresome tasks and ask for help. You should not bear the burdens of all people even if they are personal clients since this predisposes you to stress. Good interpersonal relationships are also encouraged to promote inner peace. If you are coping through drugs or alcohol, you should develop intentions to change. This is appropriate in cases where one is struggling with anxiety, depression, or other issues such as drug abuse. Become motivated so that you can develop a positive attitude toward your profession. Be committed to daily or regular exercise to relieve stress. Adequate sleep is also essential as well as developing hobbies that are not similar to the work you do daily. These measures can help address compassion fatigue completely (Allister, 2020).

The next topic is dear to my heart. Prepare yourself, because it's time to discuss burnout.

Burnout

Many individuals are not even aware that they are dealing with burnout. So what is it? Maslach and Leiter describe burnout as a state of physical, mental, or emotional exhaustion caused by prolonged or excessive individual stress. For burnout to occur, one must be drained completely either emotionally or physically and unable to carry out their normal activities as usual (Mayzell, 2020).

An individual with burnout may start to lose interest in their daily activities due to a lack of motivation. It can lead to a depreciation in productivity since they completely lack the energy to carry out the activities and they are often at the same time helpless, resentful, skeptical, or losing hope completely. These individuals feel that they have nothing to offer despite their amazing abilities and skills. As a result, burnout affects all areas including social life, homes, and working abilities (Swensen & Shanafelt, 2020). This decline in the quality of work and in both physical and psychological health can be costly—not just for the individual worker, but for everyone affected by that person.

My experience with burnout happened in 2019. I had just entered my first year of internship within my master's program. I was working full time handling multiple families in crisis situations and I was still operating full time in dance ministry. In ministry, I was coordinating weekly rehearsals, sending out weekly homework assignments, creating choreography for songs we were dancing to, and making costume decisions for what we would wear for the next song dance. In addition to this, I began learning a new position at my internship program. I was not eating healthy nor getting proper rest, and my body began to be affected. I had a hard time getting out of bed each morning. I had vomiting episodes and severe pain within my body. By the time I reached my ordination to become a pastor in October 2019, I could hardly move my body or emotionally feel anything. I was so exhausted that my husband had to take on more of the duties at home. He works full time, so coming home from work and taking on my responsibilities became frustrating for him. I thank God for him. He is so patient with me. After him having to rush me to the emergency room so many times, I had to recognize that I needed help. This is when I began focusing on my self care journey.

Symptoms of burnout are often gradual. They may be difficult to notice in the beginning until they continue to worsen. They can be mental, physical, or emotional and can impact the immune system. This can be easily observed in someone who is highly prone to frequent flu and cold infections. You might feel tired without carrying out any task. You may be drained of energy and unable to carry out activities that you could perform before (Aem, 2020). A person dealing with burnout may start experiencing repeated and frequent headaches as well as muscle cramps linked to increased levels of stress. Changes in diet may become apparent when they lose their appetite. A person suffering from burnout may experience insomnia or disturbed sleep patterns due to thinking more than usual. This person may start withdrawing from doing the duties assigned to them because they are unable to concentrate (Fansher et al., 2019). The person may isolate themselves from friends and family or project their problems to other people and at times may become hostile. They may start skipping work or reporting late. When assigned a task to carry out, it may take longer to accomplish than before. They may present with the symptom of failure and self-doubt. They may feel detached from other people, become difficult to motivate, and develop a negative attitude.

The good news is, there is hope for the treatment of burnout. Once you have recognized the symptoms of burnout, you must establish measures to help in recovery. Prevention and treatment will involve turning to other people like partners, friends and families. By being close to positive people, you will be able to share your problems and limit interaction with negatively influential people (De Looff et al., 2018). Socializing more with other people prevents feelings of loneliness. Changing the way you perceive yourself at work is also essential, which can be accomplished by creating balance in your life. Making friends at work is also important when dealing with burnout. Developing an exercise program can help reduce stress, and implementing a balanced diet promotes health and healing. Evaluating personal priorities and setting boundaries will also help do away with burnout.

These treatments can be effective in reducing stress, which will help treat burnout (Fansher et al., 2019). Providing the best care to yourself will bring about change mentally, physically, psychologically, and spiritually. This is why I am so passionate about self care. Without it, there is no way to provide effective and qualitative care to others who are in need of your service. Like my pastor says, "Self care is the best care." Schedule some time in your calendar for yourself. We all create new habits in life, so you might as well create some healthy ones. For instance, I am determined to retreat once per year at a resort and spa for several days. Getting away from daily stressors, forgetting about my responsibilities, and getting to a peaceful place can help me recognize the many human senses we possess. If you've never experienced this, I invite you to join me! If you have experienced this, then you know how refreshing it is and why you should gather with me each year. My organization comes to the aid of professional leaders and caregivers in the community by offering holistic educational and spiritual tools for self care. We provide a resort and spa experience for faith leaders to become refueled, refreshed, and pampered spiritually, physically, and emotionally so you can go back into your working field and continue to do what you do. You pour out so much, and my organization provides an environment for you to be poured back into spiritually, physically, and emotionally in Jesus' name.

Self-Care

While working as an ER CSW, I entered graduate school. During my second year in my master's program, along with working on the front lines, I was attending classes at night along with meeting assignment deadlines, and I had even more obligations. I was a dance coordinator at my local church and had just begun my first year of internship at an elementary school as an intern social worker. Beyond that, I was a mentor to others. With the multitasking of several responsibilities during that season, the stress from multiple domestic violence investigations at work began to take a toll on me physically. During that season of my life, I had grown to camouflage the way I responded to stress. Instead of talking about it or stepping away from it, I thought I could keep going no matter what my body was trying to tell me.

During one particular month, I was continuously in an out of the urgent care and the ER. While working, I had shortness of breath, the weight of pressure on my chest, dizzy spells, severe stomach nausea and pain, and migraines. There were times when I would vomit and break out into cold sweats. Every time I went to the doctor, I was told there was nothing wrong and that I needed to rest. But with my schedule, there was no time for rest. Doctor's visits would force me to take two or three days off from work here and there, and then I would jump right back in full-force. The attacks continued to increase. My body was screaming out for help and I was ignoring it. As I continued to push and push and push, the physical attacks manifested at unwelcome times. My body began to shut down, and I had gotten to a place where I was experiencing burnout.

I love people so much and I love caring for people's needs. But at the rate I was going, I realized I would kill myself if I continued to ignore taking care of myself first. We are no good to anyone else when we neglect caring for ourselves. The scripture of Matthew 22:36-39 reminds us of the greatest commandment. We are to love the Lord with all of our heart, soul, and mind. The second commandment is to love others the same way that we love ourselves. The key is the way we love. God created us in His image and likeness. We must recognize that we are a gift from God, and we must take care of that gift through the actions of love. We must love ourselves the same way we would love our neighbors.

But what exactly is love, and how do we know that we are operating out of love toward ourselves and others? This is an excellent question, and a huge topic that I'll save for another book. For now, let's focus on self care.

There are many areas of self care—psychological, social, professional, environmental, spiritual, financial, emotional, and physical (Collins, 2021). I will discuss spiritual, financial, emotional, and physical self care. Self care is any form of practice or routine that is carried out to improve levels of connection with self.

When it comes to spiritual self care, you can nurture the connection of self and a higher power. This helps to improve your faith and nourish the body and soul. Earlier, I mentioned leading while spiritually bleeding. Some of you may know what this phrase means, but for those who are hearing it for the first time, I would like to clarify what spiritual bleeding is. Spiritual bleeding is a soul that is wounded and/or broken. In the Bible, Proverbs 18:14 states that the spirit of a man will sustain his physical or mental weakness; but who can bear a wounded, broken, or angry spirit? When I hear "wounded," I think of an animal trying to be saved, but the person who tries to save the wounded animal ends up getting hurt or attacked. The wounded animal is trying to protect itself from becoming more wounded, just like a broken-hearted or angry person may deal with bitterness or unforgiveness. This form of spirit is unbearable for others to handle or be around. A leader who is leading while bleeding can be damaging to those they are leading. If you are leading while bleeding or have been hurt by people and no healing has taken place, this wounded heart can destroy your relationship with God and destroy relationships with people you come in contact with. For one to maintain spiritual care, we must think positively always and consume ourselves with knowledge that enhances our spirit. When exploring our spiritual core relationship in God, it helps to realize who we are in Christ and receive the proper healing needed when one has been spiritually wounded.

Emotional self care is being aware of how we are feeling and recognizing how our emotions affect others. It's okay to recognize your feelings. Many of us have learned to keep our feelings suppressed. Some cultures have taught our boys and men that they can't cry because it will make them look weak. We have to get out of these cliche traditions. It is so important to take care of our emotional needs. This is done through identifying one's feelings and choosing to respond in a way that cannot hurt others. To practice emotional self care, one must put their needs into consideration first, set boundaries, and understand what triggers particular emotions (Ues, 2020).

When it comes to physical self care, we must do what we can to participate in physical activities for our bodies. Our bodies weren't made to sit still. We were created to move. All my life, I've been active, but since becoming a social worker I find myself behind the computer more often and sitting for several hours at a time. Because of this, I find myself with stiff joints and less energy. Since the start of my self care journey, I have made it a priority to take at least a ten-minute walk break while at work. Physical self care helps to improve one's physical health. It may include a healthy nutritional lifestyle and regular exercise. Seeking medical care is also another contributor to good health, as well as an adequate amount of rest. This brings about mental stability for a healthy lifestyle (Green, 2017). With physical active movements, our dopamine levels increase, which allows the mind to be in a better, healthier mood (Dohrn et al, 2020). When we have a healthier mindset, we are more motivated and prepare to help those we service.

Financial self care in particular hits close to home for me. I experienced a recent situation with a person in my organization and it caused my thinking light bulb to shine bright. I have high respect for this person, and those who know me well know that I love to give to people, especially financially. Due to this person's position in the community and anointing, I placed this person in a position that was highly needed for my organization. The position paid $1,500 a month. This person was to coordinate and develop a particular team for the organization. Sparing the details, I failed at micro-managing and assumed that the goal was being accomplished. The amount was not in agreement with others in the organization, but because of my passion and my respect for this person, I was determined to make it happen. Did God tell me to do this? Looking back, I would say no. I did it all on my own. Needless to say, the person was not fulfilling what I thought was being done, and when I spoke to them about it, they took my money and quit. That mistake caused me to learn more about myself and how I relate to finances. I learned a valuable lesson after giving out close to $10,000 to this person. Had I been implementing financial self care in my life, this situation could have been avoided. I will not make that mistake again.

Some avoid the subject of finances or lack the knowledge to help, but I testify to you my situation in order to bring awareness that self care in your finances is so important and should not be ignored. Financial self care is the ability to lower financial stress levels, and it begins with a healthy and disciplined mind. One must do away with bad habits such as money misuse and take control over the money they earn (Bliz, 2020). Because of my emotional issues surrounding finances, I confess that I misused my finances because I wanted so badly to help someone else. Because of it, I lost in the end and found that this person wasn't who they portrayed to the community. It was all about the money. I praise God because where I am weak, my husband is strong. He was able to step in and take control of the situation and apply a resolution. We have been given the power to attract wealth. The Bible speaks about the topic of money more than any other subject found within the Bible. Because of this, I personally believe that God wants us to prosper in our finances. Having the knowledge to handle money is an important part of our self care.

So exactly what does the Bible say about self care? It refers to our physical body as the temple of the Holy Spirit. Therefore, we are given the authority to take care of our body spiritually, emotionally, and physically. The Bible allows for self care to help nourish our souls and take care of our health. In the book of Matthew, the Bible commissions us to speak our needs as they are continually restored in faith. Accordingly, by taking care of ourselves, we shine light on others and the world in general (Clark, 2020). Self care helps us remain strong to fight spiritual and physical battles. We as leaders become role models because of our light shining in our communities and those we impact. Self care helps us realize who we are and the kind of life we are worthy of leading (Bliz, 2020). It is a motivation tool. As leaders of faith leading by example, we are able to assist others in developing positive thinking. As a result, self care in our lives shines a bright light on many others, thus changing their ways of living. It may influence others to love life and develop an interest in living because they are inspired to live with positive intentions (Green, 2017).

I used to give and give and give until I couldn't physically function. I was disappointed with myself because I couldn't push my body past its limit. Little did I know, I was trying to pour from an empty cup. This is when I came to the reality that "no" was a good word. Using it taught me to create healthy boundaries. When I was afraid to say "no," I ended up exhausted because I would take on too much to handle. After becoming repeatedly ill, my physical body forced me to learn the word "no," and to say it with confidence. People in my life took advantage of my kindness, and looking back, I've realized that I gave more grace than what was required. I am not God, and I must understand that I can't fix things or resolve situations for everyone. We live and learn, and as we have breath in our bodies, we will continue to learn new lessons in life. Because my passion is serving others, I know I will have plenty more lessons that I will end up learning.

Where do we go from here? I would like to invite you on an exciting self care adventure.

A Call to Action

Thanks to my life experiences, I have a deep understanding of stress and burnout. I can distinguish between good stress and unhealthy stress, and at times I can sense stress in other people as well. I'm on a mission to illustrate the love of Jesus and also to push faith leaders in understanding the high standards of self care. I'm here to assist those who are feeling stuck to move into their full potential. I am sensitive to the needs of others and so compassionate in this, and I sincerely believe that my purpose is to serve leaders in these needs.

Times of Expression & Refreshing (TER) Ministries was born from my pain. TER Ministries is a 501c3 nonprofit organization with a mission to serve faith-based leaders with self care strategies and resources. We provide a safe atmosphere with monthly virtual live events performed for the purpose to further educate faith leaders in self care strategies. Annually, we provide in-person retreat and spa conferences for leaders to be pampered. We focus on spiritual self care, physical self care, and financial self care. We have partners who provide further educational tools and access to help when needed. You are on the front lines, and you need someone who will have your back through those trying times of leading while bleeding, or when your cup is running low. We want to prevent you from the risks of vicarious trauma, secondary traumatic stress, compassion fatigue, and burnout.

Our annual retreats are great keys to self care. Every year, we hold a pampering experience in a different state within the US. Staying connected is important! I need you to know that you are not alone. We need each another. Proverbs 27:17 teaches that one person can sharpen another person. This allows connection and networking for each of us to be better in who we are and what we do as faith leaders. This is why we must sharpen one another and why the mission of TER Ministries is so important. What better way to sharpen but through a retreat and spa conference? An important part of self care is retreating from stress and the busyness of life.

I can hear you saying, "I don't have time for stuff like that." But you must create time for yourself. Feel free to create a list of excuses why you can't attend a resort event. You can try and talk yourself out of it if you want to, but you are cheating yourself of replenishment. Just as you pour out to others, you also need to be poured into. What good is a cup with nothing in it? Time away gives you the opportunity for the Lord to anoint your head with oil so that He is able to pour back into you all that you've poured out to others.

Your cup will begin to overflow. Giving yourself permission to engage in self care will upset some people, but that's okay. When you take time to become a better you, others will thank you for it. Being aware of your own needs will help you better serve others. We each need balance in life, and you've been leading while bleeding for long enough. As my pastor tells us, "I want you to live long and live strong."

Thank you for reading this book. It's so important to know the information I've outlined here. It's time to be aware of the signs and symptoms created from trauma and learn how to heal from it. It is my sincere prayer that you may prosper and be in good health as your soul prospers. In Jesus' name!

We have partners and affiliates ready to serve you in your self care journey. If you feel called to our mission and would like to become an affiliate, please don't hesitate to reach out to us at email: info@terministries.com. If you desire to be pampered each year, let's stay connected! Go to www.terministries.com and check out who we are and why we do what we do. On our website, you will find the information needed for the annual retreats we host every year. We will keep you updated with annual events and details on how to prepare for them ahead of time. To receive updates via email, take your phone out and aim your camera at the QR code below. We look forward to fellowshipping with you soon!

Giving Back

A portion of proceeds from book sales will be donated to TER Ministries 501c3 charitable nonprofit organization.

References

Aem J. (2020). undefined. Everything You Need to Know About Caregiving for Parkinson's Disease, 39-45. https://doi.org/10.2307/j.ctv15wxnsd.16

Allister, R. (2020). Compassion fatigue: What is it and how can you help? BSAVA Congress Proceedings 2020, 250-251. https://doi.org/10.22233/9781910443774.30.2

Bliz. (2020). Care homes and financial abuse. Financial Abuse of Older Clients: Law, Practice and Prevention. https://doi.org/10.5040/9781784515522.chapter-05f

Clark, E. (2020). Book review: Soul care in African American practice. Journal of Spiritual Formation and Soul Care, 13(2), 319-321. https://doi.org/10.1177/1939790920963484

Collins, S. (2021). Social workers and self-care: A promoted yet unexamined concept?. Practice, 33(2), 87-102.

Crowe, L. (2016). Identifying the risk of compassion fatigue, improving compassion satisfaction, and building resilience in emergency medicine. Emergency Medicine Australasia, 28(1), 106-108. https://doi.org/10.1111/1742-6723.12535

De Looff, P., Didden, R., Embregts, P., & Nijman, H. (2018). Burnout symptoms in forensic mental health nurses: Results from a longitudinal study. International Journal of Mental Health Nursing, 28(1), 306-317. https://doi.org/10.1111/inm.12536

Del, F. I. (2019). Compassion fatigue: A heavy heart hurts. Compassion Fatigue and Burnout in Nursing. https://doi.org/10.1891/9780826155214.0006

Dohrn, I. M., Papenberg, G., Winkler, E., & Welmer, A. K. (2020). Impact of dopamine-related genetic variants on physical activity in old age–a cohort study. International Journal of Behavioral Nutrition and Physical Activity, 17, 1-8.

DuBois, A. L., & Mistretta, M. A. (2019). Compassion fatigue. Overcoming Burnout and Compassion Fatigue in Schools, 59-76. https://doi.org/10.4324/9781351030021-5

Fansher, A. K., Zedaker, S. B., & Brady, P. Q. (2019). Burnout among forensic interviewers, how they cope, and what agencies can do to help. Child Maltreatment, 25(1), 117-128. https://doi.org/10.1177/1077559519843596

Figley, C. R. (2013). Compassion fatigue: Coping with secondary traumatic stress disorder in those who treat the traumatized. Routledge.

Figley, C. R. (2017). Encyclopedia of trauma: An interdisciplinary guide. SAGE Publications.

Figley, C. R. (2018). Compassion fatigue: Coping with secondary traumatic stress disorder in those who treat the traumatized. Routledge.

Gley, G. L. (2016). Traumatic stress: The management of secondary traumatization and comorbidity.

Gottfried, R., & Bride, B. E. (2018). undefined. Encyclopedia of Social Work. https://doi.org/10.1093/acrefore/9780199975839.013.1085

Green, M. J. (2017). Global justice and health: Is health care a basic right? Public Health Policy and Ethics, 203-221. https://doi.org/10.1007/1-4020-2207-7_12

Konistan, R. (2017). The effects of secondary trauma on professionals working with victims and survived traumatized individuals.

Lcsw, S., & Sawicki, S. (2019). Mental health workers' vicarious trauma, secondary traumatic stress, and self-care.

Lodha, P. (2021). Interventions for the management of vicarious trauma among mental health professionals during COVID-19.

Maslach, C., & Leiter, M. P. (2016). Burnout. In Stress: Concepts, cognition, emotion, and behavior (pp. 351-357). Academic Press.

Mayzell, G. (2020). What is burnout: "The disillusioned physician syndrome". The Resilient Healthcare

Organization, 11-20.
https://doi.org/10.4324/9780429286025-2

Miller, B. C. (2021). Reducing secondary traumatic stress: Skills for sustaining a career in the helping professions.

Sprang, G. (2018). Vicarious trauma redefining PTSD. Social Work.
https://doi.org/10.1093/obo/9780195389678-0267

Sprang, G., Ford, J., Kerig, P., & Bride, B. (2019). Defining secondary traumatic stress and developing targeted assessments and interventions: Lessons learned from research and leading experts. Traumatology, 25(2), 72.

Steele, W. (2019). Reducing compassion fatigue, secondary traumatic stress, and burnout: A trauma-sensitive workbook.

Swensen, S. J., & Shanafelt, T. D. (2020). undefined. Mayo Clinic Strategies To Reduce Burnout, 211-212.
https://doi.org/10.1093/med/9780190848965.003.0027

Taithe, B. (2019). Compassion fatigue. Emotional Bodies, 242-262.
https://doi.org/10.5622/illinois/9780252042898.003.0012.

Ues F. (2020). Emotional needs of people with dementia and their care partners. Fast Facts for Dementia Care.
https://doi.org/10.1891/9780826151810.0010.

Watts, M., & McAfee, M. (2021). VICARIOUS TRAUMA AND IMPLICATIONS FOR SOCIAL WORK STUDENTS.

www.ingramcontent.com/pod-product-compliance
Lightning Source LLC
Chambersburg PA
CBHW050448010526
44118CB00013B/1738